# Prince Fielder

By Jeff Savage

AMAZING ATHLETES

⌐ Lerner Publications Company • Minneapolis

Lerner Publications Company
A division of Lerner Publishing Group, Inc.
241 First Avenue North
Minneapolis, MN 55401 U.S.A.

Website address: www.lernerbooks.com


Library of Congress Cataloging-in-Publication Data

Savage, Jeff, 1961–
    Prince Fielder / by Jeff Savage.
        p.    cm. — (Amazing athletes)
    Includes index.
    ISBN 978–0–7613–8668–1 (lib. bdg. : alk. paper)
    ISBN 978–0–7613–8916–3 (eBook)
    1. Fielder, Prince, 1984– 2. Baseball players—United States—Biography. 3. African American baseball players—Biography. I. Title.
    GV865.F4268S28 2012
    796.357092—dc23 [B]                                               2011030752

Manufactured in the United States of America
1 – BP – 12/31/12

# TABLE OF CONTENTS

Prince Fielder gets ready to bat at Comerica Park on October 18, 2012.

# PRINCE OF DETROIT

First baseman Prince Fielder stood in the **batter's box** at Comerica Park in Detroit. Thousands of fans buzzed in the stands.

Millions more were watching on TV. Prince stepped forward and took a mighty swing at the baseball. He made contact and sent the ball into right field for a hit.

Prince and the Detroit Tigers were leading the New York Yankees, 1–0. It was the third inning of the fourth game of the 2012 **American League Championship Series (ALCS)**. The Tigers had won the first three games of the series. If they could win this game, Detroit would go to the World Series.

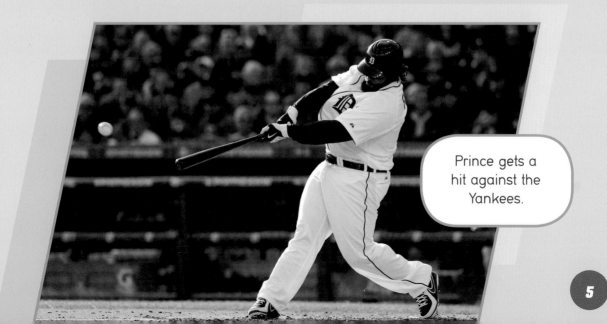

Prince gets a hit against the Yankees.

Prince moved up to second base. Then he ran to third base. Prince's teammate Avisail Garcia came to bat. Garcia hit the ball to the left side of the field. Prince ran home to score Detroit's second run

The New York Yankees are the most successful team in **Major League Baseball (MLB)** history. They have won the World Series 27 times.

of the game. The Tigers had the lead, 2–0.

Detroit scored four more runs in the fourth inning to take a 6–0 lead. New York scored a run in the sixth to make it 6–1. The Tigers scored two more times. The score was 8–1 when New York came to bat in the ninth inning. The Yankees needed seven runs to tie the game.

New York hitter Jayson Nix came to bat with two outs in the inning. He swung hard and popped the ball high into the night sky. Prince moved beneath the ball and waved his arms. He shouted, "I've got it!" to his teammates. Prince caught the ball and raised both arms above his head. He jumped up and down and celebrated. The crowd roared. The Tigers were going to the World Series!

Prince *(second from left)* holds onto the ball for the final out of the ALCS.

"There's a long way to go but this is an awesome feeling," Prince said after the game. The Tigers were happy to beat the Yankees. But they knew that winning the World Series was the biggest prize. "Four more wins, guys," said Detroit third baseman Miguel Cabrera. "Four more wins." Could the Tigers beat the San Francisco Giants in the World Series?

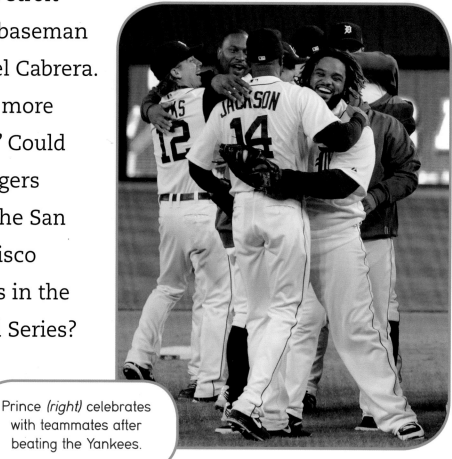

Prince *(right)* celebrates with teammates after beating the Yankees.

Prince *(left)* at home with his father, Cecil *(right)*; mother, Stacey *(center)*; and baby sister, Ceclynn, in 1993.

# FUN DAYS

Prince Semien Fielder was born May 9, 1984, in Ontario, California. He lived with his parents, Stacey and Cecil. He has a younger sister named Ceclynn.

The family lived in different towns around the country. Cecil was a power-hitting first baseman in the major leagues. He led MLB in home runs as a member of the Detroit Tigers in 1990 and 1991. He won the World Series in 1996 with the New York Yankees. He also played for the Toronto Blue Jays, the Anaheim Angels (now known as the Los Angeles Angels of Anaheim), and the Cleveland Indians.

Prince's father said Prince was sure to become a baseball player. "The game is in his blood," said Cecil. "Since he was one year old, wearing a diaper, he had a bat in his hand."

Prince was a large boy. By the age of two, he weighed nearly 50 pounds. He had a big appetite. Prince was teased in school for his weight. But his classmates also thought he was cool for having a famous dad.

When school was out for the summer, Prince joined his father on road trips. Players wrestled with Prince and gave him candy in the locker room. He went to the houses of superstars like Ken Griffey Jr. and Derek

Prince joins his dad in the Detroit Tigers locker room in 1993.

Jeter. "Those were the fun days," Prince said.

Prince played Little League baseball. He had a mighty swing. He hit his first home run at the age of 10. "I didn't see it. I was running hard," said Prince. The ball went over the fence. "When I got to second base, the **shortstop** said, 'You hit a homer.'"

Prince often got to take **batting practice** before his father's games. In 1996, he hit his first home run at Tiger Stadium. He was 12. "Prince was unbelievable," said former Tigers player Al Kaline. "When he played against kids his own age, it was like a man against boys."

Prince began high school at Florida Air Academy in Melbourne, Florida. He wanted to be a pro baseball player. But Prince weighed 300 pounds as a sophomore. He knew he had to lose weight.

Prince started running and lifting weights. He lost 50 pounds in two years. He bashed monster home runs as a senior at

Prince wearing his high school baseball uniform

Eau Gallie High School in Melbourne. One ball sailed out of the park and crashed through a gas station window across the street. For the season, Prince had a .524 **batting average** with 13 **doubles** and 10 homers.

**Scouts** thought Prince had a chance to play in the major leagues. The Milwaukee Brewers selected him with the seventh pick of the 2002 MLB **draft**. Prince received a $2.4 million **signing bonus**.

Prince *(right)* talks to his dad before batting practice with the Milwaukee Brewers in 2002.

Prince *(right)* played first base for the Beloit Snappers in 2003.

# TRYING TO FOCUS

Prince tore through the Brewers **minor-league** teams. He hit .390 with 10 home runs for the **rookie** league Ogden Raptors in 2002. Prince moved up to the Class A Beloit Snappers after just 41 games.

Prince was walking off the field after a game with Beloit when a man came up to him. The man was looking for Prince's father. Cecil was in trouble. He owed millions of dollars from bad business decisions. He also lost a lot of money gambling. Cecil hid from the people that wanted money from him. "Prince was embarrassed," said his close friend Tony Gwynn Jr.

Cecil's money problems lasted for more than a year. Prince's mother and father divorced. Prince and his father got into shouting matches. "I was worried about [Prince]," said Gwynn. "He was a wreck."

Tony Gwynn Jr. *(right)* and Prince became close friends while playing for the Snappers.

Prince found peace on the baseball field. "All that stuff, it went away when I was on the field," he said. "I just got to play baseball and not think about it." Prince stopped speaking to his father in 2004. "My father is dead to me," he told a newspaper reporter.

By 2005, Prince was playing for the Class AAA Nashville Sounds. He was hitting .291 with 28 homers when the Brewers called him up to the big-league club in August. He was the sixth-youngest player in the majors.

The Brewers named Prince their new first baseman. He was nervous. In his first four games of the 2006

Prince worked hard to get stronger. MLB scouts were impressed. "I sat there amazed," said Milwaukee Brewers scout Tom McNamara. "Prince really showed his hunger to succeed."

Prince started slow in 2006 but soon found his groove.

season, he failed to get a hit. He struck out seven times. Prince relaxed and began bashing the ball. "I have high expectations," said Prince, "so hopefully I just keep getting better."

Prince batted over .300 in July. He hit his 18th home run to break the team rookie record. "He's got a chance of being a leader on our ball club, a special player," said Milwaukee general manager Doug Melvin. "Our players see how hard he plays."

Prince poses with his wife, Chanel, and sons, Jadyn *(left)* and Haven *(right)* in 2011.

Prince had recently married his girlfriend Chanel and started a family. "For the first time in a long time everything is calm in Prince's life," said Gwynn. "He can focus on baseball. And he can focus on his family, raising his kids. He wants to be a great father."

Prince *(right)* celebrates a home run with teammate Ryan Braun.

# BECOMING A LEADER

Prince became the Brewers team leader in 2007. "As a rookie, you just shut up," he said. "I had fun last year, but I tried to be quiet, do my job, and pay my dues." Prince inspired his teammates by having fun. "Everybody here is in love with him," said **veteran** catcher Damian Miller. "Once you hear him laugh, you can't help but laugh, too."

Prince was a dangerous hitter. In May 2007, he hit six homers in 11 games. A month later, he was named the starting first baseman for the **All-Star Game**. He got more votes than former Most Valuable Players (MVPs) Ryan Howard and Albert Pujols. "He's a special kid," said Brewers manager Ned Yost. "He's fearless and he plays with passion. He's a superstar."

Prince hit his 46th home run in September to set a team record for homers in a season. "He's a dangerous, dangerous young man," said Cincinnati Reds manager Dusty Baker.

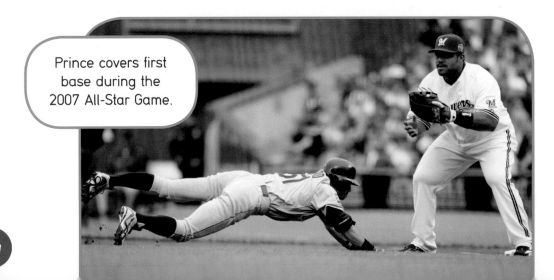

Prince covers first base during the 2007 All-Star Game.

Ten days later, Prince became the youngest player ever to reach 50 homers in a season. Prince and his father became the only father-son combination in major-league history to each hit 50 homers in a season.

Prince tips his helmet to cheering fans after hitting his 50th home run in 2007.

In 2008, Prince hit an **inside-the-park home run** against the Toronto Blue Jays. He hit a **walk-off homer** against the Pittsburgh Pirates in late September. The Brewers finished the season with a 90–72 record. They made the **playoffs**. It was Milwaukee's first trip to the playoffs since 1982.

The Brewers faced the Philadelphia Phillies. In Game 4, Prince hit a home run. Unfortunately, it was the only homer for the Brewers in the series. Milwaukee lost in four games.

Prince was wildly popular. He appeared on the cover of magazines. He was voted to the 2009 All-Star Game in St. Louis. He competed in the **Home Run Derby** and hit 17 home runs in the first two rounds. One of his homers went 503 feet.

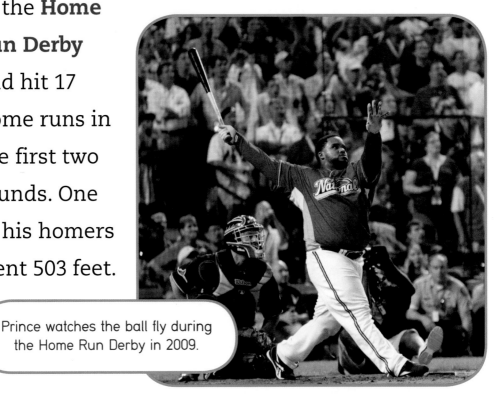

Prince watches the ball fly during the Home Run Derby in 2009.

He clubbed six more in the final round to win the Derby. His two sons, Jadyn and Haven, ran onto the field to give him big hugs.

Prince continued to bash the ball. But the Brewers struggled to win in 2010. Prince was upset. The team signed him to a **contract** for $15.5 million to play one more season. It was the richest single-season deal in history. But it meant Prince would become a **free agent** after 2011. He could join any other team. Would Prince leave Milwaukee?

Prince is a vegetarian. He does not eat meat or fish. His wife gave him a book that described how animals become food. Prince became a vegetarian after reading the book.

Prince runs the bases after hitting a three-run homer during the 2011 All-Star Game.

# SUPERSTAR

Prince's teammates loved being with him. "We leave it to him to crack us all up," said teammate Rickie Weeks. "He can remember every quote from every movie."

On the field, Prince kept up his hot hitting and was chosen for the 2011 All-Star Game.

Prince came to bat in the fifth inning. The AL led, 1–0. Prince's team had two runners on base. Could Prince come through with another big hit? He swung hard at the pitch. He sent the ball high toward centerfield. It hit off the top of the wall and bounced over for a three-run homer! The National League won the game, 5–1. Prince was named MVP of the game.

Prince holds the MVP trophy on his shoulders after the All-Star Game in 2011.

The Brewers played well in 2011 and made the playoffs. They beat the Arizona Diamondbacks in the first round. But Milwaukee's season ended in the next round against the St. Louis Cardinals. The Cardinals would go

Prince knocks in a run against the Arizona Diamondbacks during the 2011 playoffs.

on to win the World Series. "We were real, real close this year," said Prince's teammate Nyjer Morgan after losing to the Cardinals.

Attention turned to Prince as soon as Milwaukee's season ended. He was now a free agent and could sign with any team that wanted him. Rumors swirled that Prince would join the Los Angeles Dodgers. Others said he was going to the San Francisco Giants. Most people were surprised when Prince agreed to sign a contract with the Detroit Tigers in January 2012.

Detroit already had a good team. Prince and Tigers' slugger Miguel Cabrera are two of the best hitters in baseball. "It's awesome," Prince said. "I really don't know what to say. I just never thought this could happen, and it's happening now. It's an awesome moment." The Tigers signed the big first baseman to a nine-year contract worth $214 million.

Prince says people shouldn't compare him to his father. "We both laugh a lot, but other than that we are totally different," says Prince. "He is more laid-back. He could joke around on the field, but I am all serious."

Prince quickly showed that he was worth the money. He had a .313 batting average in 2012 and 30 home runs. The Tigers had the best record in the **AL Central Division** and went all the way to the World Series. But they lost in four games to the San Francisco Giants.

Prince has become one of the game's most feared hitters. But he's still a favorite in the locker room. He isn't a flashy player. "I just try to do my part," said Prince.

Prince slides home during the 2012 World Series.

# Selected Career Highlights

**2012**  Signed a contract with the Detroit Tigers

**2011**  Named the All-Star Game Most Valuable
Player
Hit a three-run homer for the NL in the All-Star
Game

**2010**  Ranked sixth in the NL with 32 home runs
Ranked third in the NL with a .401 on-base percentage

**2009**  Won the All-Star Home Run Derby
Led the NL with 141 runs batted in
Set the Brewers team record for runs batted in
for a single season
Ranked second in the NL with 46 home runs
Ranked second in the NL with a .602 slugging
percentage
Hit his first career grand slam against the Cleveland Indians

**2008**  Led the Brewers to their first playoff appearance in 26 years
Ranked eighth in the NL with 34 home runs

**2007**  Led the NL with 50 home runs
Became the youngest major-league player ever to hit 50 home runs
in a season
Won the Silver Slugger award as the best offensive first baseman in
the NL
Named to the All-Star Game
Ranked third in the NL with 119 runs batted in

**2006**  Named the NL Rookie of the Month in April
Led major-league rookies with 28 home runs

**2005**  Batted .291 with 28 home runs and 86 runs batted in for Class AAA
Nashville
Named to the *Baseball America* Class AAA All-Star Team

**2004**  Batted .272 with 23 home runs and 78 runs batted in for Class AA
Huntsville

**2003**  Batted .313 with 27 home runs and 112 runs batted in for Class A
Beloit

**2002**  Drafted in the first round by the Milwaukee Brewers

# Glossary

**AL Central Division:** one of the three groups of teams that make up the AL. The AL Central is made up of the Chicago White Sox, the Cleveland Indians, the Detroit Tigers, the Kansas City Royals, and the Minnesota Twins.

**All-Star Game:** a game held midway through the Major League Baseball season featuring the best players in each league

**American League Championship Series (ALCS):** a set of games played at the end of the baseball season between the top two teams in the American League. The team that wins four games goes to the World Series to play the winner of the National League Championship Series (NLCS).

**batter's box:** the rectangular area on either side of home plate in which a batter stands while at bat

**batting average:** a number that describes how often a baseball player gets a hit

**batting practice:** an activity before a game in which players practice their swing by hitting pitches

**contract:** a deal signed by a player and a team that states the amount of money the player is paid and the number of years the player plays

**doubles:** hits that allow batters to safely reach second base

**draft:** an event in which teams take turns choosing new players

**free agent:** a player who is free to sign a contract with any team

**Home Run Derby:** a contest held the day before the All-Star Game in which hitters compete to hit the most home runs

**inside-the-park home run:** a home run in which the ball does not go over the wall, yet the batter is able to circle the bases and cross home plate without being tagged out

**Major League Baseball (MLB):** the top group of professional men's baseball teams in North America, divided into the National League and the American League

**minor league:** a professional league below the major leagues where players gain experience and improve their skills

**playoffs:** a series of games held every year to decide a champion

**rookie:** a player playing his or her first year

**scouts:** people who judge the skills of players

**shortstop:** a player who plays in the field between second base and third base

**signing bonus:** a sum of money given to a player as a reward for signing a contract

**veteran:** a player with experience

**walk-off homer:** a home run that is the last swing of the game and wins the game

## Further Reading & Websites

Fishman, Jon M. *Miguel Cabrera*. Minneapolis: Lerner Publications Company, 2013.

Kennedy, Mike, and Mark Stewart. *Long Ball: The Legend and Lore of the Home Run*. Minneapolis: Millbrook Press, 2006.

Savage, Jeff. *Justin Verlander*. Minneapolis: Lerner Publishing Company, 2013.


Detroit Tigers: The Official Site
http://www.detroit.tigers.mlb.com
The official website of the Detroit Tigers includes the team schedule and game results, biographies of Prince Fielder and other players and coaches, and much more.

Major League Baseball: The Official Site
http://www.mlb.com
The official website of Major League Baseball includes schedules, game results, late-breaking news, and biographies of players like Prince Fielder, and much more.

*Sports Illustrated Kids*
http://www.sikids.com
The *Sports Illustrated Kids* website covers all sports, including baseball.

# Index

# Photo Acknowledgments

The images in this book are used with the permission of: © Leon Halip/
Getty Images, pp. 4, 5; REUTERS/Mike Cassese, p. 7; © Mark Cunningham/
MLB Photos/Getty Images, p. 8; © Taro Yamasaki/Time & Life Pictures/Getty
Images, p. 9; © Michael Zagaris/Getty Images, p. 11; Seth Poppel Yearbook
Library, p. 12; AP Photo/Morry Gash, pp. 13, 19; © John Zich/CORBIS, p. 14;
© G. N. Lowrance/Getty Images, p. 15; AP Photo/Darren Hauck, p. 17;
© Rich Pilling/MLB Photos/Getty Images, p. 18; REUTERS/Mike Blake, p. 20;
© Allen Frederickson/Reuters/CORBIS, p. 21; © Jamie Squire/Getty Images,
p. 22; © Christian Petersen/Getty Images, pp. 24, 25; © Jared Wickerham/
Getty Images, p. 26; © Doug Pensinger/Getty Images, p. 28; © Thearon W.
Henderson/Getty Images, p. 29.

Front cover: © Otto Greule Jr/Getty Images.

Main body text set in Caecilia LT Std 55 Roman 16/28.
Typeface provided by Adobe Systems.

# XTREME SCREAMS

# THE WORLD'S MEANEST
# Monsters

**A&D Xtreme**
BOLD HI-LO NONFICTION

An imprint of Abdo Publishing
abdobooks.com

## S.L. HAMILTON

# TAKE IT TO
# THE XTREME!

### GET READY FOR AN XTREME ADVENTURE!
### THE PAGES OF THIS BOOK WILL TAKE YOU INTO THE THRILLING
### WORLD OF THE MEANEST MONSTERS ON EARTH.
### WHEN YOU HAVE FINISHED READING THIS BOOK, TAKE THE
### XTREME CHALLENGE ON PAGE 45 ABOUT WHAT YOU'VE LEARNED!

THIS BOOK CONTAINS
RECYCLED MATERIALS

Editor: John Hamilton; Copy Editor: Bridget O'Brien
Graphic Design: Sue Hamilton
Cover Design: Laura Graphenteen
Cover Photo: iStock

Interior Photos & Illustrations: Alamy-pgs 34-35; AP-pgs 16 (inset) & 30-31; Cartoon Network-pg 41 (bottom); Dave Rubert-pg 44 (inset); DC Universe-pg 37 (bottom); Getty-pgs 9, 21 (inset) & 26-27; Gustave Doré-pg 36; Hanna-Barbera-pg 41 (top); iStock-pgs 1, 4-5, 8, 14-15, 18-19, 20-21, 22-23, 24-25, 37 (background) & 44; Legendary Pictures-pg 39 (inset); NASA-pg 1 (Moon); Radio Pictures-pg 38; Scholastic-pg 37 (middle); Science Source-pgs 16-17 & 25 (top); Sega-pgs 42-43; Shutterstock-pgs 6-7, 10-11, 12-13 & 28-29; The History Channel-pg 40; Toho Co.-pg 39; Warner Bros-pg 42 (inset); Wordsworth Editions-pg 37 (top).

**LIBRARY OF CONGRESS CONTROL NUMBER: 2020948034**

**PUBLISHER'S CATALOGING-IN-PUBLICATION DATA**

Names: Hamilton, S.L., author.

Title: The world's meanest monsters / by S.L. Hamilton

Description: Minneapolis, Minnesota : Abdo Publishing, 2022 | Series: Xtreme screams | Includes online resources and index.

Identifiers: ISBN 9781532194856 (lib. bdg.) | ISBN 9781644946237 (pbk.) | ISBN 9781098215163 (ebook)

Subjects: LCSH: Monsters--Juvenile literature. | Monsters in mass media--Juvenile literature. | Monsters in popular culture--Juvenile literature. | Monster films--Juvenile literature.

Classification: DDC 398.2454--dc23

# TABLE OF Contents

# CHAPTER 1
# THE WORLD'S MEANEST
## Monsters

Monsters are described as big, frightening creatures that attack humans. Most are created in legends and stories. But some are thought to live in the wild. People wonder if they are real or **imaginary**.

## XTREME FACT

**Cryptozoologists are people who search for creatures that have not been proven to be real.**

# CHAPTER 2

# History

When people began exploring the world, they encountered creatures they had never seen before. Some maps warned: "Here be dragons."

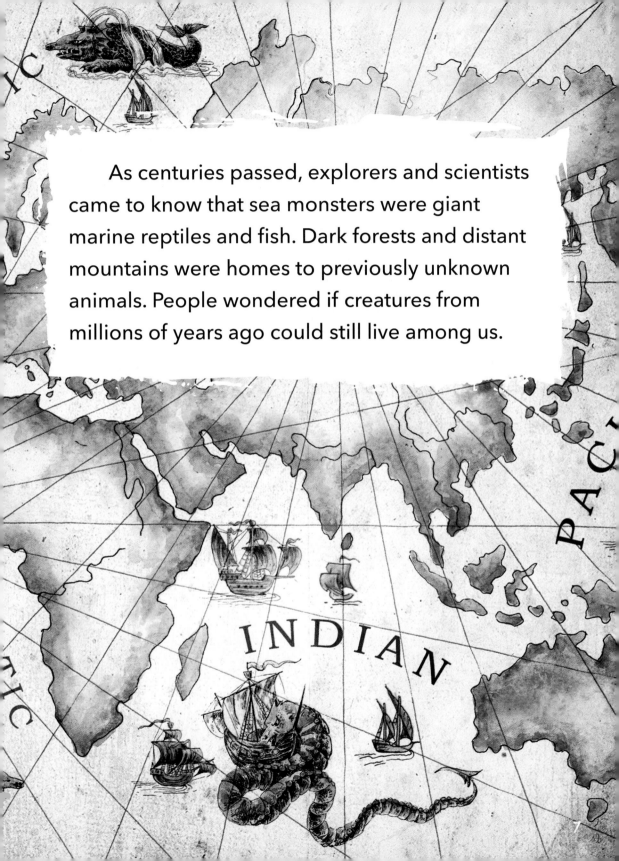

As centuries passed, explorers and scientists came to know that sea monsters were giant marine reptiles and fish. Dark forests and distant mountains were homes to previously unknown animals. People wondered if creatures from millions of years ago could still live among us.

# CHAPTER 3

# Monster Sightings

**Caution Sasquatch Sightings**

**Protect Your Park**
No Tree-Cutting
Or
Trail-Building

Hundreds of people claim to have seen a furry, apelike creature. Known as Bigfoot, or Sasquatch, it is said to hide in forests and swamps of the United States and Canada. None have been brought back, dead or alive. Other than blurry photos, there is no proof this monster lives.

## XTREME FACT

**Bigfoot is described as 7-10 feet (2-3 m) tall and weighing up to 500 pounds (227 kg). People also say that they hear a grunting or screeching sound and smell a horrible odor.**

A still frame from a 1967 film shot by Bigfoot-seekers Roger Patterson and Bob Gimlin. People thought it was real until Bob Heironimus came forward 35 years later. He was hired by the two men to wear the Bigfoot suit. The footage was fake.

From the Himalaya Mountains come tales of a humanlike monster known as the yeti, or Abominable Snowman. Many explorers have searched for the **elusive** creature.

Giant footprints have been discovered in the snow. Some thought they were made by a yeti. Scientists believe the tracks were just distorted animal prints that enlarged by melting and refreezing.

A 1951 photo of a giant footprint, taken by explorers in the Himalayas.

For centuries **mariners** told tales of a giant sea creature called Leviathan. It made the sea boil. Steam hissed from its nostrils and clouds of smoke rose from its mouth. Some thought it was a monster. Others believe it may have been a blue whale. Adults weigh 150 tons (136 metric tons) and spout water 40-50 feet (12-15 m) in the air.

Blue whales are the largest animals on Earth.

Norse myths tell of the kraken. The huge creature could **engulf** and sink an entire ship. Sailors feared a kraken's attack. Some thought it was a sea monster, while others believed it was a giant octopus or squid.

15

In April 1934, a doctor took a photo of what appeared to be a sea creature swimming in Scotland's Loch Ness. The deep lake would be a perfect hiding place for a long-necked marine reptile. Some thought it was an ancient **plesiosaur**.

The Surgeon's Photo, as it was called, seemed like proof that Nessie lived. However, at the time, many people thought the image was an otter or marine bird.

The search for "Nessie," the Loch Ness monster, went on for decades. Finally, in 1994, it was discovered that the photo was actually a toy submarine fitted with a clay sea monster head. Many people still wonder if some kind of sea creature is living in Loch Ness's dark waters.

Many cultures have tales of dragons. Mexico's Quetzalcoatl is a winged serpent-god. Europe's legends tell of Saint George killing a dragon that demanded **human sacrifices**. Asian dragons bring good luck and are thought to be kind and wise. The stories may have arisen from fierce, real reptiles.

Quetzalcoatl

**Dragons have many different looks. Some have two legs and some four. Some fly with magic and others with wings. Some breathe fire or poisonous gas. Some are good and others are evil.**

Saint George kills an evil dragon.

Africa has stories of a monster with a long neck, an alligator-like tail, and the body the size of an elephant. It is called Mokele-mbembe. Its name means "one who stops the rivers." Some believe it to be a **sauropod** dinosaur. Others say it's an elephant swimming with only its trunk and the top of its head showing.

A swimming elephant may look like Mokele-mbembe.

## XTREME FACT

In 1992, a Japanese film crew flying over Lake Tele, Congo, captured 15 seconds of what they thought might be Mokele-mbembe. The blurry film shows something leaving a large V-shaped wake as it swam.

Kongamato is described by African natives of western Zambia as a beaked, flying reptile. Some believe it to be a pterosaur, a creature that died out 65 million years ago. Reports of a flying demon with a wingspan of 4-7 feet (1-2 m) and a mouthful of teeth continue to make people wonder if the monster really survived the ages.

Pterosaurs had arms and bodies covered in stretched skin. Some think the flying reptile might have survived to modern times.

Chupacabra is a mysterious monster seen in Puerto Rico, Mexico, Nicaragua, Chile, and the southern United States. Some say it has sharp teeth, red eyes, and pointed quills running down its back. Others believe the monster may have been a stray dog, an aye-aye, or humans playing **grisly** tricks. Still, some claim chupacabra is real.

Chupacabra means "goat sucker." It was named when an unknown creature drained the blood from several dead goats.

The rare aye-aye is native to Madagascar.

# CHAPTER 4

# Real Monsters

Some "monsters" are really just monster-sized animals. Many snakes grow to amazing sizes. One record-breaking python measured 49 feet (15 m). That's longer than a city bus! Pythons have even been known to consume children and small adults.

Reticulated Python

A Komodo dragon hunts for prey using its forked tongue to pick up chemical molecules in the air and on the ground.

Indonesia's Komodo dragons are the largest living lizards in the world. They can grow as big as 10 feet (3 m) in length. They eat all types of meat, from eggs to water buffalo.

These real-life dragons are deadly. A bite from a
Komodo dragon sends huge amounts of **bacteria** into
its prey's bloodstream. This causes death within a week.

Giant squid live deep in the ocean, but sometimes come to the surface to hunt food. These huge creatures can grow up to 50 feet (15 m) in length. They have been known to attack small ships.

A real giant squid hangs in Paris's French National Museum of Natural History. It is preserved with a special resin.

## XTREME FACT

Giant squid are so big they have been mistaken for floating islands.

The giant Pacific octopus is the largest species of octopus in the world.

The largest recorded giant Pacific octopus weighed 600 pounds (272 kg) and had an arm span of 30 feet (9 m) across. With 2,000 powerful **suckers** and a biting, parrotlike beak, it is easy to see how **mariners** might think of them as sea monsters.

# CHAPTER 5

# MONSTER HUNTING
# Equipment

A thermal image of someone in a Bigfoot costume shows how a heat-detecting device can help locate a monster.

People look for **elusive** monsters all around the world. Some search in remote areas and many use heat-detecting devices. The most important equipment is a video or still camera to clearly document the creature.

# CHAPTER 6
## MONSTERS
# In the Media

Monster stories have been told for centuries. Whether from authors' **imaginations** or real-life creatures, books are filled with tales of wild beasts.

**One of the earliest books, *The Bible*, tells of God destroying a Leviathan.**

In 1869, science fiction author Jules Verne wrote *Twenty Thousand Leagues Under the Sea*. His tale of adventures and sea monsters is still read today. It has been made into comic books, movies, and games.

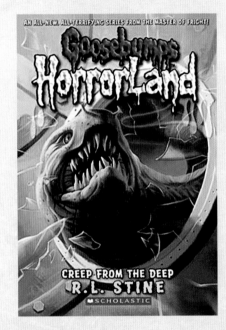

R.L. Stine's Goosebumps HorrorLand series has several monster stories, including *Creep from the Deep*.

The DC Comics series *Gotham City Monsters* features hero characters from Monstertown, including Frankenstein, Killer Croc, and Orca.

Monster movies bring adventure and scares to viewers. RKO Radio Pictures' 1933 *King Kong* was one of the first major monster films. The 25-foot (8-m) -tall gorilla was called the "Eighth Wonder of the World." The famous monster continues to star in movies, books, and games.

## XTREME FACT

In the 2017 film *Kong: Skull Island*, King Kong was **100 feet (30 m) tall**. **That's taller than the tallest dinosaur that ever lived.**

KING KONG

with
FAY WRAY · ROBT. ARMSTRONG
BRUCE CABOT    A COOPER-SCHOEDSACK
                        PRODUCTION
FROM AN IDEA CONCEIVED BY
EDGAR WALLACE AND MERIAN C. COOPER

Godzilla was created for a 1954 movie. Awakened by atomic testing, the giant, lizard-like monster attacks a city in Japan. Godzilla has been in so many movies, it was once the longest-running **film franchise**. *Godzilla: King of the Monsters* came out in 2019, and more movies are planned.

The original Godzilla's special effects are called "suitmation." Godzilla was a man in a reptile suit destroying a miniature city.

Monsters are seen in many TV shows. The History Channel's *MonsterQuest* searched for a variety of creatures. Cartoon monsters are sometimes fierce and sometimes friendly.

*MonsterQuest* **searched for information on monsters, such as Mothman.**

Jonny Quest took on a yeti and other monsters in the 1964-1965 series.

In *Monster Beach*, a brother and sister go to an island occupied by quirky, surf-loving monsters and an evil witch doctor with tiki minions.

Video games often feature fearsome monsters. In some, players fight the evil creatures and in others, they are the monsters. The skills and challenges are fun and exciting!

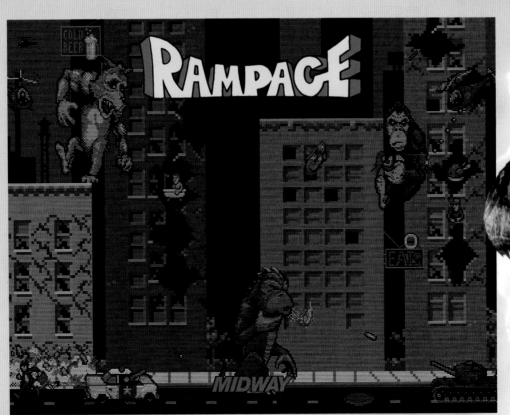

*Rampage* first came out in 1986. Players control one of three monsters: a werewolf, a lizard, or a giant gorilla.

**DANGER**

**10,000 VOLTS**

**Players of *Jurassic Park: The Lost World* video game fight their way through many monster dinosaurs that inhabit the island.**

# CHAPTER 9

# Are Monsters Real?

Many people claim to have seen monsters. But most have turned out to be fake. Without bodies, bones, **scat**, or tissue samples, it's impossible to prove. Clear photos or video footage helps. What is seen in the dark, or in rain or fog, can trick a person. Most monsters are fictional stories.

**Stompers used to create Bigfoot tracks.**

# XTREME
# Challenge

**TAKE THE QUIZ BELOW AND
PUT WHAT YOU'VE LEARNED TO THE TEST!**

1) What phrase was printed on early maps to warn sailors of areas where sea monsters might be found?

2) What are two names for a furry, apelike creature that is said to live in North America's swamps and forests?

3) A Leviathan is a sea monster that sailors feared. What do scientists think it really was?

4) What kind of monster is a kraken?

5) Scotland's "Nessie" was photographed in 1934. But what was really in the doctor's Loch Ness photo?

6) Name two dinosaur-age monsters that people think might still be alive in areas of Africa.

7) What fictional monster was called the "Eighth Wonder of the World"?

8) What would be proof that a monster is real?

# Glossary

**bacteria** – Single-celled organisms that multiply rapidly and break down living tissue. Bacteria often cause sickness, and sometimes death, in animals and humans.

**elusive** – Someone or something that is hard to find or catch.

**engulf** – Wrap around or surround something completely.

**film franchise** – A series of related films all produced around a central character or characters.

**grisly** – Something awful that causes horror or disgust.

**human sacrifice** – The killing of a person or persons as an offering to a god, spirit, ruler, or supernatural power, in order to protect the rest of the people or tribe.

**imaginary** – Not real. Pretend.

**mariner** – A sailor.

**plesiosaur** – A long-necked, small-headed sea reptile that swam in Earth's oceans 200 million to 65 million years ago, during the Mesozoic era. The name plesiosaur means "near lizard." When first discovered, it was thought that the bones were from an ancient lizard.

**sauropod** – The largest of the plant-eating dinosaurs. They lived during the Mesozoic era, from about 245 million to 65 million years ago. As the biggest land animals to ever live, they weighed as much as 100 tons (91 metric tons) and stood more than 40 feet (12 m) tall.

**scat** – Animal droppings or poop.

**suckers** – Shallow, cup-shaped organs that hold fast to an object. An octopus's tentacles have rows of suckers that are used to hold and taste their prey.

# Online Resources

**Booklinks**
**NONFICTION NETWORK**
FREE! ONLINE NONFICTION RESOURCES

To learn more about the world's meanest monsters, please visit **abdobooklinks.com** or scan this QR code. These links are routinely monitored and updated to provide the most current information available.

# Index